The End of the Cow

And Other Emerging Issues

Will You Be Cared for by a Robot?
Will You Be Taught by a Hologram?
Will We Stop Eating Meat?

Table of Contents

1   EMERGING ISSUES ANALYSIS   1

2   THE ANTICIPATORY CITY   9

3   DISRUPTING THE COW   21

4   WOMEN REALLY LEAD THE WAY   29

5   THE CHANGING FAMILY   41

6   LEARNING ANYTIME, ANYWHERE, WITH ANYONE   53

7   AUTHORS   65

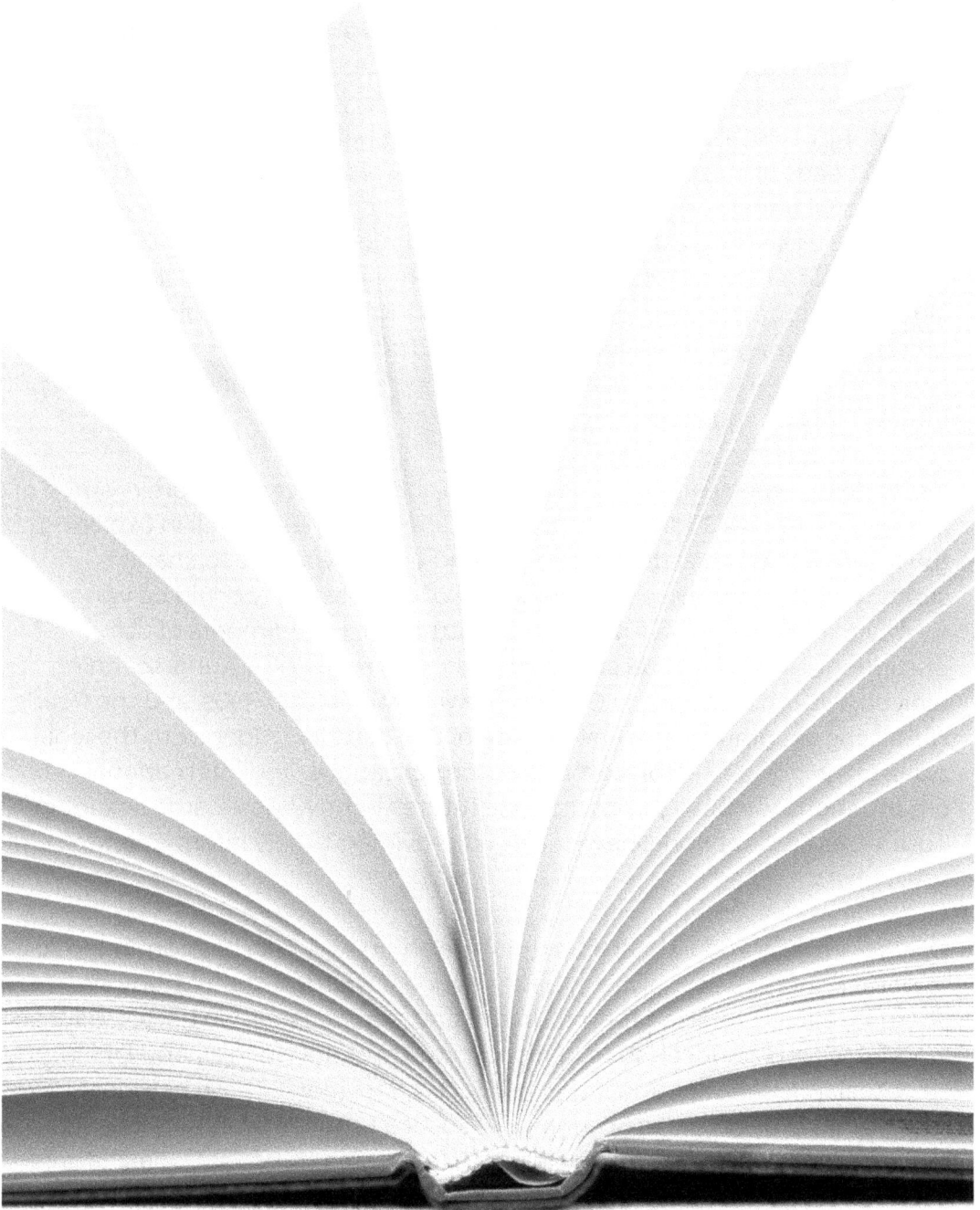

Foreword

My (Sohail) first exposure to futures scanning/emerging issues analysis was in the late 1970s. Professor James Dator, one of the founders of Futures Studies, was explaining the work of Graham Molitor, the utility of seeing problems through the lens of the S-curve. He suggested that through this approach, we could identify problems before they became unwieldy, track who is ahead and who is behind on global policy issues and use the method to develop more robust and informed choices at personal and organizational levels. Later, as an intern with the Hawaii Judiciary, we were given the opportunity to use emerging issues analysis to better meet the changing judicial needs of citizens. Over a decade, we explored and developed reports on the legal rights of robots, the possibility of Hawaiian sovereignty, emerging brain drugs, the shift toward mediation and meditation, and the possibility of a Federal Constitutional Convention. While robots do not have legal rights today, reports on that issue, were impactful in helping see the present as remarkable, as contested, indeed, as malleable. Emerging issues began to be seen not just as a method to better understand the emerging future but to change today.

In the 1980s, emerging issues analysis took off and became a core method of not just the Hawaii Judiciary, but other state judiciaries as well in exploring the future. Sometimes they were bold and used the future to change strategy, and other times as Dator spoke of, the best they could do was go twenty minutes into the future. The institutional impediments of using disruptions to create novel strategies was too great. Still, futures scanning took off, with the Singapore Courts following suit in the 1990s, and the Pearls of Policing program in the first decade of this century. Along with the legal system, the private sector, community organizations, and international organizations too have jumped on the futures bandwagon. Large scanning businesses and networks have taken off providing timely information to subscribers.

Our work (Ivana and Sohail) at Metafuture.org in Australia has continued to use emerging issues analysis as a foundational method in the study of alternative and preferred futures. In the past two decades we have produced lengthy reports for local, state, national governments (such as Abu Dhabi, New Zealand, Canada), and international organizations. These have included reports with titles such as Scanning for Justice Futures, Scanning for Correctional Futures, Scanning for City Futures, Scanning for Social Futures in Asia, Scanning for Health Futures, Ageing Societies and the Youth Bulge,

Changing Worldviews and Food Futures, the Futures of Culture and Tourism, University Futures, and Infrastructure 2050-70.

This scan itself was originally written for a number of groups including international health organizations and a national parliament. The ideas have been tested in repeated foresight exercises.

We hope you find it of use whether for personal interest, in developing business strategy, in developing national strategy, in shaping international policy decisions, or in other ways you can see to use the future to better understand our tomorrows and more effectively shape today.

Sohail Inayatullah and Ivana Milojević
February, 2022
Brisbane, Australia

Emerging Issues Analysis

Emerging issues analysis (EIA) seeks to identify threats and opportunities – issues – before they become unwieldy and expensive to act on. The method also seeks to identify bellwether localities where new social innovation starts (the future in the present). EIA is used to scan the environment, to discover issues that lie beyond the horizon. These issues tend to have low evidence - marginal support in the literature - but with a potentially high impact if they move from being a seed of change to a full-fledged tree or forest. They are anomalous issues, which some commentators have called *black swan*s (Talib, 2008). Seongwon Park of the Korean National Parliament Assembly calls these *cracks in the wall* (2021, December 16, personal email). They could bring the house down or could, if acted upon early enough, buttress the safety of the home. Staying with this analogy, cognizance of the emerging issue could lead to a redesign of the home.

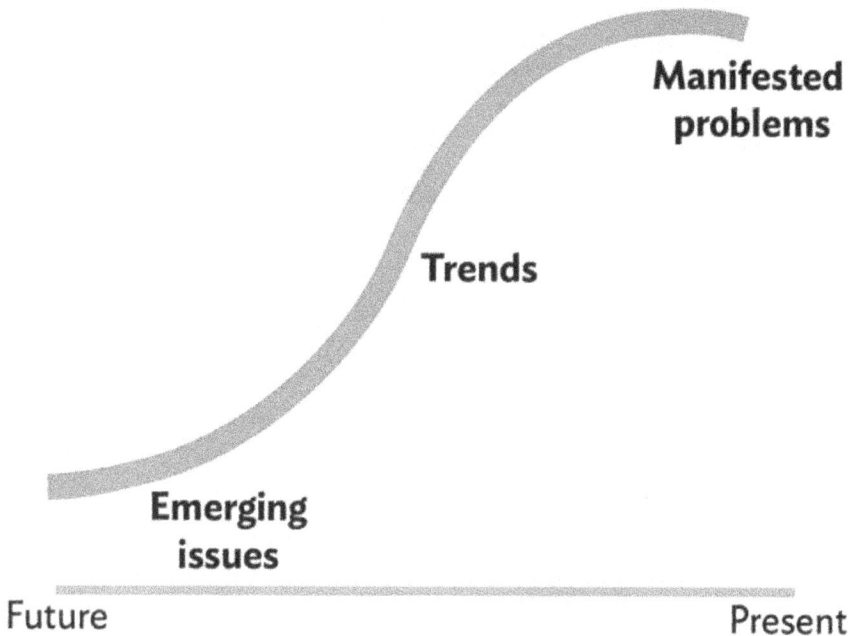

Future   Present

Emerging issues analysis was first developed by Graham Molitor in the late 1950s, published in a seminar research paper in 1977, and championed by James Dator (1980), one of the pioneers of the field of Futures Studies in his work for the US legal system in the 1980s and 1990s.

Using the S-curve, Molitor identifies three phases of an issue. The first, at the bottom left of the S-curve, it is generally unknown. Over time, if it has traction, the issue (citations, articles, comments, laws, conferences) moves up the S-curve becoming a trend. It then attracts attention from leading think-tanks. Finally, it moves from nascent possibility to reality, becoming an issue that is debated in public media and legislatures with decisions needing to be taken.

For example, thirty or so years ago there were discussions on cellular agriculture – as a solution to climate change, as part of the rise of the vegetarian movement, as a more efficient way to produce protein. Today, there are numerous corporations that have developed products for sale globally. Some nations are ahead in developing policy, in seeding funding for this innovation (some are even developing the "Internet of Food", food as software), while others are dealing with the immediate issues of hunger and food justice.

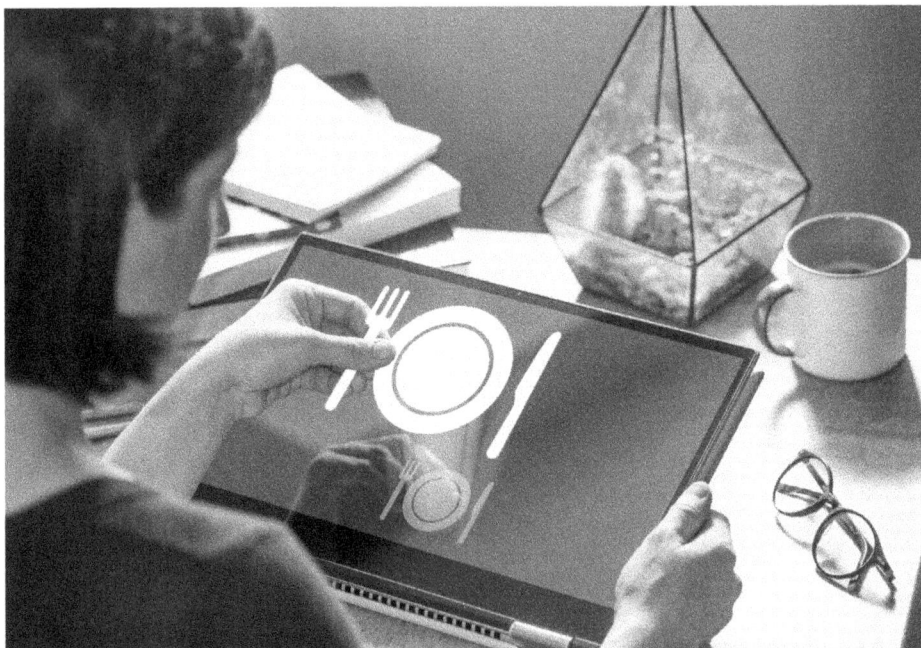

While aspects of cellular agriculture are now a trend – initial products and articles, books, conferences, businesses having sprouted up – in some areas of the world, other aspects of the "disruption of the cow" remain beyond the horizon. A particular emerging issue, even if it does not come to fruition, can for the researcher spark discussions that lead to novel and different emerging issues. One can thus track organizations as well as nations on the S-curve in terms of their adoption of a particular issue. While those ahead lead, those behind can watch and learn and make decisions based on more data. But which issues are useful or relevant?

Writes Dator, first discussing the framing of the issue (2018: 6):

Examples of emerging issues are typically displayed as follows: (1) if it is relevant and reasonable to do so, by giving a date by which the issue will have significant social, environmental, and/or physical impact, and then (2) by titling the issue in a straightforward declarative statement with no immediate explanation or justification.

However, merely fitting into the worldview of the organization, while efficient, does not lead to change, argues Dator (2018:6):

The intention is to provoke disbelief, puzzlement, perhaps shock, even disgust—not immediate acceptance and agreement. It is only after an emerging issue has been so stated, and then some evidence for it has been given, that (3) the stated impact is explained via one or more scenarios that show possible developments of the issue from its first emergence to its significant impact.

Questioning Reality

While sensitive to this approach, we focus more on if it disturbs current categories of reality and if it challenges the paradigms of stakeholders. If it does not, then the organization in question remains fixated on the present, unable to see the possibilities beyond the horizon. This means in effect making the present remarkable, using the emerging issue not as a forecasting or foresight method per se but to challenge the current paradigm.

For example, research we conducted in the early 1990s on the emerging issue, the legal rights of robots, transformed from the novelty of possible occurrence to debates on what part of the legal system can be automated. Resultant issues and consequences could see the elimination of much of what attorneys do or could create more time for reflection for judges. While robots certainly do not have rights per se today, as we enter the metaverse, more and more legal battles on human-robot interaction (human robot marriage, the rise of robot brothels and the end of sex trafficking) are likely to emerge (Inayatullah and Na, 2018). Emerging issues thus not only help in tracking weak signals and events, but they can also challenge the very notion of what constitutes an event, a data point. They need to challenge the pre-understandings of decision makers, using the unthinkable to challenge the normal (Inayatullah, 2004). Wayne Yasutomi (1981) has suggested that emerging issues should not only be tracked through weak signals but also through conversations with those on the margins of society: shamans, and others outside the disciplinary grids of society.

Emerging issues analysis or scanning for the unusual is a foundational part of futures-orientation, futures literacy. Standing in contrast is problem-oriented planning. In this approach, the problems facing the system are collected and prioritized by the stakeholders. The utility of this approach lies in the fact that the functional efficiency of the system increases; however, structural problems (meta-problems) are often not noticed and gains are often for the short-term. Emerging issues analysis also differs from political-oriented planning. The latter is focused on issues that lead to electoral gain, ensuring that the political administration uses discourse and narrative to stay in political power. However, emerging issues analysis is futures-oriented in that it is focused on the long-term. As well, it helps create a map of possible futures. It uses novelty to challenge the current normal. It forces policymakers to focus on what can be, how the emergent can be used to find new business, social, and political opportunities. It is both warning-based – what can go wrong – and opportunity-based – how to leapfrog the current system for future competitive advantage.

An emerging issue needs to have some text orientation (a scientific experiment, a new product, some articles, news writings, interviews of experts) and while not plausible, needs to be shown to be relevant in the future. It also cannot be overly general (aliens landing in the future), but rather specific and plausible (by 2040, 50% of all protein will be derived through in-vitro meat). Emerging issues, thus defined, are what-if questions with some basis to them. The basis is made up of weak signals, evidence in the literature of the anomalous. Of course, many potential emerging issues will not emerge (flying cars for all) or will emerge at a point where they are no longer useful for decision makers. However, the purpose of the issues can be to change the framework of national strategy: for example, moving the debate from car energy efficiency (electric cars) to mobility (driverless cars, or uber cars for all, or walking cities). Emerging issues are thus used to help understand new ways of seeing reality, so novel policy solutions can be crafted.

Therefore, emerging issues analysis needs to be situated within a worldview perspective. In a world where information leads to enhanced policy-making and strategy, EIA can provide lead time to avoid certain futures and create other futures. By keeping us alert to weak signals, EIA can spark discussions on new opportunities. Moreover, even if the emerging issue is not exactly on the mark, it can lead to an understanding of other emerging issues as the organization becomes more futures literate: imagine a series of cascading s-curves each holding the potential for disruption. However, in a world where decision-making and planning is political – that is not information-based, but tribal/identity-based – then emerging issues, especially those presented as warnings, are likely to be ignored as futures orientation is not relevant. Leaders will continue to engage in futures fallacy after futures fallacy as present concerns overwhelm the needs of the future (Milojević, 2021), until it is too late. This is so for problem-based planning as well. Current problems might be successfully solved but the system (organization, nation, institution) will always be behind, always catching up to innovation elsewhere. This enhances the chance of being disrupted or epistemologically colonized.

Emerging issues analysis thus seeks to not just enhance foresight but also seeks to disrupt our understandings of today and tomorrow so new narratives and preferred futures can be created.

For the Practitioner

For the practitioner, there are several useful approaches.

First, one can take a particular emerging issue and track its development over the past decades, to see how it has changed or stayed the same. This maps the traces of the issue.

Second, one can populate the S-curve with emerging issues, trends, and current problems along topic areas: for example, energy futures, or transportation innovation, health futures or food safety.

Third, after choosing an emerging issue, one can populate the far left of the s-curve with weak signals, article citations, and comments by thought leader proponents.

Finally, after emerging issues analysis, it is best if one uses the Futures Wheel (Glenn, 1972). This develops first and second order implications, and resultant scenarios.

For this booklet, we have selected five domain categories. They are:

1. The Anticipatory City
2. Disrupting the Cow
3. Women Really Lead the Way
4. The Changing Family
5. Learning Anytime, Anywhere, with Anyone

References and Further Reading

Dator, J. (1980). *Emerging issues Analysis in the Hawaii Judiciary.* Honolulu: The Hawaii Judiciary.

Dator, J. (2018). Emerging Issues Analysis: Because of Graham Molitor. *World Futures Review,* 10(1): 5-10.

Glenn, J. (1972). Futurizing Teaching vs. Futures Courses. *Social Science Record,* 9(3): 26-29.

Inayatullah, S. (2008). Six Pillars: Futures Thinking for Transforming. *Foresight,* 10(1): 4-21.

Inayatullah, S. (2004). *The Causal Layered Analysis Reader.* Tamsui: Tamkang University.

Inayatullah, S., & Na L. (2018). *Asia 2038: Ten Disruptions That Change Everything.* Tamsui: Tamkang University.

Milojević, I. (2021). Futures Fallacies. *Journal of Futures Studies,* 25(4): 1-16.

Molitor, G. (1977). How to Anticipate Public Policy Changes. *SAM Advanced Management Journal,* 42 (Summer): 4-13.

Molitor, G. (2003). *The Power to Change the World.* Maryland: Public Policy Forecasting.

Silver, N. (2012). *The Signal and the Noise.* London: Penguin.

Talib, N. (2008). *The Black Swan.* New York: Random House.

Yasutomi, W. (1981). *Emerging Issues Analysis.* Honolulu: The Hawaii Judiciary.

The Anticipatory City: creating wellness and wellbeing

The Anticipatory City: will the city of the future be preventive, able to provide early indicators of illness and wellbeing?

KEY MESSAGES

- Traditionally the core functions of the city have been about roads, rates, and rubbish. The future city is likely to be anticipatory, a living and complex adaptive system that is focused on individual and collective wellbeing.

- The measurement of what counts in cities is likely to shift from commercial activity, a single bottom line focused on infrastructure projects to a quadruple bottom line, focused on prosperity, people, planet and wellbeing.

- This shift in the city will be created by: 1. The possibility of new artificial intelligence technologies. 2. New sensing technologies – the internet of everything, living building, eyes, and ears everywhere. 3. Cities embarked on visioning alternative and desired futures, and 4. The peer-to-peer health model focused on participation and partnership.

- This is captured by the 5P model: prevention, precision, prediction, participatory, and partnership.

- However, the anticipatory city could just as well lead to a totalitarian society. This could be where individual liberties are severely curtailed for the collective good or the use of these new technologies for electoral/political control. It is thus critical that this is not just a continuation of the smart city paradigm but the shift to a peer-to-peer citizen-led paradigm, even moving toward a Gaian vision of the polity.

Signals of Change

There is already some initial success in using artificial intelligence to analyse social media data to "capture longitudinal environmental influences contributing to individual risk for suicidal thoughts and behaviours" (Roy, 2020). An algorithm called "Suicide Artificial Intelligence Prediction Heuristic" (SAIPH) has been invented to anticipate suicide using data from Twitter (Roy, 2020).

A Japanese city, Otsu, has begun experimenting with AI to predict how suspected cases of school bullying could evolve into the future. This was a result of a bullied boy killing himself in 2011. They argue that "If AI is able to prevent even one student from reaching the same breaking point as that boy in 2011, this new initiative will be well worth the effort – and perhaps it'll even inspire other schools across the globe to create similar AI systems to protect their own students." (Houser, 2019).

There are numerous efforts by cities to become futures-oriented, to use the tools of Futures Studies to create their alternative and preferred futures (Russo, 2016; 2017).

There are also business and technical discussions on using sensors throughout the city, connecting hundreds of billions of devices, what has been called the world of a trillion sensors with an economic impact of 3.9 $ trillion to 11.1 trillion $. (McKinsey, 2015). The shift will require interoperability, security, enhancing the use of current predictive technologies, and linking all the devices with significant gains for health systems (Sentence, 2021).

There is also considerable innovation by the corporation Ali Baba to create what is called the City Brain. The City Brain now is functioning in 29 cities in the West Pacific. Initial success in Hangzhou is remarkable (Alibaba Cloud, 2019). More concretely:

- Travel time on the original congested 22-kilometer Zhonghe-Shangtang elevated highway has been reduced by 4.6 minutes on average.
- Only 2.6 seconds is required to pass a pay station at any pilot parking lot without a traditional barrier gate.
- Hangzhou is the first city to be able to flexibly control vehicles with non-local licenses. Local Hangzhou residents can apply for 12 digital passes for each non-local vehicles every year. A digital pass allows a visit to travel with non-local vehicles in what are restricted areas during any restricted access period in Hangzhou.
- Checking in and out of hotels only requires 30 seconds on average with the help of ET City Brain.
- Digital pass cards eliminate queues for parks, with there being only a 20 seconds wait time on average before entry.
- The idea of "Treat first, pay later" is coming to fruition, with medical treatment paid after fact, saving on average 1 hour from the doctor visit.
- ET City Brain have helped ambulances arrive at destination 7 minutes faster on average.

If we take this current success and begin to imagine if current trends continue, by 2030 and certainly by 2040, the City Brain could lead to the true Anticipatory City. (Alibaba Cloud, 2019)

Taking the above changes as a point of departure, the main argument is that cities move from being passive to becoming agents of health change. For example (Inayatullah, 2009):

With increasing scientific evidence that city design directly impacts our life changes and our long-term health, city planners are redesigning for health. City design improvements include creating greener and more bio-diverse spaces to enhance psychological health – bringing in light rail to reduce congestion (time spent in traffic directly relates to heart disease), changing zoning to reduce pollution (in polluted areas fetus size drops) and of course with climate change here and on the horizon, rethinking population density zoning. Enhancing green spaces can also reduce drought as there is considerable evidence that the suburban/strip mall model of development blocks billions of gallons of rainwater from seeping through the soil to replenish ground water. Rethinking city design can greatly reduce costs over the long term. Building design is part of this revolution, creating cradle to cradle buildings with zero emissions where there is no way to throw things. Energy self-reliant buildings are on the cards. Green buildings, while costing more initially, enhance productivity.

The anticipatory city would link devices, wearables, "implantables", and "digestables," to smart buildings, smart eco-systems and a create a new governance infrastructure to manage these devices. The devices could be used to give early warning signals of illness, prevent illness, monitor illness, and create wellness regimes. They could thus be used to enhance wellness. The value comes from linking devices to humans to specialists and to AI systems. They require a governance architecture and a strong security framework (INTERPOL, 2018).

An earlier example of issues around the digital (health) revolution at a workshop for the Ministry of Health in Bangladesh suggested that the key is not just the technology but the change in narrative. It would be a shift from "moving the patient, to moving the data" (Sheraz, Inayatullah, and Shah, 2013). An advanced Internet of Things (IOT) of health would allow the nation to leapfrog other health systems. There would also be a critical power element in that using the Grameen Bank model, the local case worker, generally female, would take responsibility of early diagnostics. However, over time, each person would have some control over their own health futures, designing systems that would support their health journeys.

An executive group in Bangkok imagined the smart and green buildings with community shared spaces. They used the CLA methodology to map today and tomorrow. CLA focuses on four areas: the observable litany, the system that underlies it, the worldview, and the core myth/metaphor (Inayatullah and Milojević, 2015).

CLA BANGKOK	TODAY	2030
Litany description	A place where people live	A place to enjoy – smart garden, smart technology, living anticipatory systems
The system	Functional space, budget based	Smart living and growing through shared community spaces
The worldview	Profit and speculation	Quality of life, first
The myth-metaphor	Student dormitory	The Bodhi building – living my life at the right place

Their conclusion was the creation of the Anticipatory city needed to be a step-by-step process with changes in the litany/data (how we measure reality), changes in the city-building infrastructure system, changes in the worldview and changes in the core metaphor of building design.

Four to Five P

As the city redesigns itself, the health framework would concomitantly shift. Earlier signs of this have been the work of Leroy Hood, who has suggested a change to the four P model. This is defined as preventive, personalized, predictive, and participatory (Hood, 2013). This is the convergence of systems medicine and the digital revolution along with the rights of the patient. To this we can add the fifth P, which is partnership (Inayatullah, 2020: 538):

The 5p model consists of: (1) Prevention (exercise, meditation, early check-ups); (2) Precision/personalized medicine; (3) Predictive health; (4) Participation (patients designing their health journey); and (5) Partnership (all agencies working together). Done well, this vision would dramatically reduce costs. It would do so by focusing on individuals in the context of their communities, use advanced genomics medicine to tailor health solutions for the individual, predict an individual's health pathway, work with patients so they could participate in their health decisions, and create health systems that work in partnership with each other. This challenges the generic, silo based, problem-solving hospital health model.

The anticipatory city requires a partnership of patients, health planners, digital platforms, security agencies, political leaders, community groups, and others.

This approach moves us from (Hood, 2013):

- Reactive to Proactive
- Disease treatment to Wellness maintenance and creation
- Population-based to Individual-based
- Records fragmented to Records on the cloud and linked
- Large scale diffusion to the Peer-to-peer health – social health
- The City as inert to the City as active

Russo adds to this debate that the approach needs to be person tailored but also life stage tailored. As he concludes on the vision of healthcare in Australia (Russo, 2019):

By 2030, the connection between personal, household, and local to global health systems will be helping more Australians to access the services they need at the right times and stages in their lives. Every health activity will have its own digital health platform to help engage people regularly and in light of all goals at each level of our health system. The real-time connection between preventative health measures and cost savings converted back into better infrastructure, equipment, services, and programs will become better known.

In a workshop with the community managed mental health service provider Mind Australia, participants suggested that the key to the anticipatory city was a shift from individuals and health systems living in a world of roadblocks to creating the digital data tree. For insurance companies, they need to shift from "generic illness insurance" to "we create the healthier you." It thus is in their interest to be a critical partner in creating the anticipatory city as their costs would go down.

CLA MENTAL HEALTH	TODAY	2030
Litany description	GDP	Wellbeing
The system	Unconnected devices/sensors, stakeholders, visions and projects. Corporatized and government-led health.	An interconnected digital ecology of connected devices, sensors, stakeholders, visions, and projects. The 5 P model.
The worldview	Reactive	Anticipatory
The myth-metaphor	A world of roadblocks	Creating the data tree

The Gaian City

In the long run, however, we can imagine the city not merely as physical infrastructure but, indeed, as a living entity i.e., Gaian – a complex adaptive system that learns from its components (humans, nature, and technologies) and evolves (Daffara, 2021a). The data collected through trillions of sensors could help city planners identify in real time new diseases and thus monitor and act. The city – seen as living – would mount defences against diseases, whether changing work patterns, accelerated contact tracing or alerting administrators to where medical specialists would need to be. In the long run, the administrators would become a design team, as in AI systems would play the monitoring and alerting dimension of the living city. Citizens are a central part to this transformation in that they become part of the collective intelligence, i.e., this moves the debate from the smart city to the collective intelligent city (Ramos, Uusikyla, and Luong, 2020). Barcelona has spearheaded attempts to use peer to peer power to transform power relations and create new forms of ownership (Smith and Martin, 2020). They argue for a shift from technopolis to a citizen-led polis through citizen debates, proposals, budgets, and plans. This helps ensure that the anticipatory does not become the technocratic authoritarian city. Ultimately, this is about creating a city based not on the values of the smart city, but the values of empowerment based on collective intelligence. This intelligence is not an end state. As they write (Smith and Martin, 2020):

Capabilities are valued appropriate to building the platform as a common endeavor belonging to all participants. This conceptualization of technology, built through participatory social relations, is key to platform success, because digital platforms for urban democracy are – like democracy itself – a perpetual work in progress.

Cities that engage in this process would have competitive advantage over those that do not, in that they will have designed for wellbeing and wellness. Productivity would be higher and citizens from around the world would wish to learn from and be part of the wellbeing revolution, from my illness to my health to our health. To use another metaphor, if we see information about individuals as a mirror, today, the mirror is stupid, merely reflecting the person. In the future, it would be a living mirror, providing health advise to the person. The mirror would also be preventive, suggesting exercise routines, diet, visits to experts. The mirror would also be linked to the city brain, assisting the individual as to where to travel and where not to travel (based on the individual's needs). The mirror would play a role not just in optimizing individual health but enhancing collective wellbeing.

Stages of the New City

Thus, there are clear stages ahead:

1. The current city. Millions of devices but not connected. Health outcomes are individual based. Prevention occurs through corporate and governmental programs. Cities tend to be reactive, seeing their roles as narrow. Data is privately owned. Insurance companies are key players.
2. The smart interconnected city. Use of smart technologies to reduce inefficiencies and enhance productivity. Devices – sensors – connected. Information is shared. Government, business, citizens, and community work on prevention. Partnerships creates health benefits. Health costs go down. Personal and collective health is enhanced. Primary health care becomes more accessible (Kelly et al. 2020). This is the beginning of the 5 P model.
3. The collective intelligent city. Sensors plus peer-to-peer governance. The 5 P model is implemented. Sensors are linked with peer-to-peer networks. Coordination and anticipation are critical to anticipation. There are major public health and financial gains.
4. The anticipatory city – the city that solves tomorrow's health problems today. AI learns and invest appropriately. Early and advanced diagnostics. Humans gain the cost and health benefits from real time anticipatory information. Data is cooperatively owned.
5. The Gaian polity – the living city. Reflective systems. Anticipation leads to emancipation.

In each phase, connectivity keeps on increasing, participation of citizens keeps on increasing, anticipation keeps on increasing, total costs to the system over time decrease, and well-being for all increases.

However, at one of these stages there are inflection points, points of divergence. Health outcomes may only go to the elites if pricing is high or if technocratic paradigms gain supremacy or if citizens lose trust in the process and technology. This would create a scenario of High-Tech Anomie, with class divisions heightened as health benefits go to the few (Inayatullah, 2004). University health care is certainly a must to drive the anticipatory city. Ensuring that data is secure and cooperatively owned will be critical in the move toward the transformed city and health system.

References and Further Reading

Alibaba Cloud (2019, October 28). *City Brain now in 23 Cities in Asia*. https://www.alibabacloud.com/blog/city-brain-now-in-23-cities-in-asia_595479

Daffara, P. (2021). *A Case for the Spiritual City (Part 1)*. [Post]. LinkedIn. https://www.linkedin.com/pulse/case-spiritual-city-part-1-dr-phillip-daffara-phd/

Daffara, P. (2021a). *The Gaian City Vision of Planetary Civilization (Part 3 of the Case for a Spiritual City)*. [Post]. LinkedIn. https://www.linkedin.com/pulse/gaian-city-vision-planetary-civilisation-part-3-case-daffara-phd/?trackingId=ZdjOqKb5603YC1MCfBaroA%3D%3D

Hood, L. (2013). Systems Biology and P4 Medicine: Past, Present, and Future. *Rambam Maimonides Medical Journal,* April 30, 4(2).

Houser, K. (2019, February 9). A Japanese City is Using AI to Prevent Youth Suicides: The Tech Could Help Teachers Intervene Before it's too late. *The Byte,* https://futurism.com/the-byte/school-bullying-artificial-intelligence.

Inayatullah, S. (2004). Cities Create their Futures. *Journal of Futures Studies,* 8(3): 77-81.

Inayatullah, S. (2009). Creating the Prama Prevention Society. *The Health Advocate,* 2. December: 24-27.

Inayatullah, S. (2020). Using the Future in Different Waves. In J. Schroeter (Ed.), *After Shock* (pp. 534-542) . New York: John August Media.

Inayatullah, S., & Milojević I. (Eds.). (2015). *CLA 2.0*. Tamsui: Tamkang University.

INTERPOL. (2018, February 22). *Internet of Things cyber risks tackled during INTERPOL Digital Security Challenge*. https://www.interpol.int/fr/Actualites-et-evenements/Actualites/2018/Internet-of-Things-cyber-risks-tackled-during-INTERPOL-Digital-Security-Challenge

Kelly, J., Campbell, K., Gong, E., & Scuffham, P. (2020). The Internet of Things: Impact and Implications for Health Care Delivery. Journal of Medical Internet Research, (22)11.

McKinsey (2015). The Internet of Things: Mapping the Value Beyond the Hype. Seoul: McKinsey Global Institute.

Roy, A., et al. (2020). A Machine Learning Approach Predicts Future Risk to Suicidal Ideation from Social Media Data. *Digital Medicine,* (78)3. https://www.nature.com/articles/s41746-020-0287-6

Ramos, J., Uusikyla, I., & Luong, N.T. (2020, April 3). Triple-A Governance: Anticipatory, Agile, and Adaptive. *Journal of Futures Studies,* https://jfsdigital.org/2020/04/03/triple-a-governance-anticipatory-agile-and-adaptive/

Russo, C. (2016). Mapping Planning and Engagement Systems Applied by Four Queensland City Futures Initiatives. *Journal of Futures Studies,* 21(2): 1-20.

Russo, C. (2017, March 2). Here's What Smart Cities do to Stay Ahead. *The Mandarin,* https://www.themandarin.com.au/76259-heres-smart-cities-stay-ahead/

Russo, C. (2019). Creating Preferred Futures of Australian Health Care. *Journal of Futures Studies,* 24(1): 101-108.

Sentence, R. (2021, January 19). *7 Examples of how the Internet of Things is Facilitating Healthcare.* https://econsultancy.com/internet-of-things-healthcare/

Sheraz, U., Inayatullah, S., & Shah, A. (2013). E-health Futures in Bangladesh. *Foresight,* 15(3): 177-189.

Smith, A., & Martin, P.P. (2020). Going Beyond the Smart City? Implementing Technopolitical Platforms for Urban Democracy in Madrid and Barcelona. *Journal of Urban Technology,* (28)1: 311-330.

99

Disrupting the Cow: the transition to cellular agriculture

Disrupting the Cow: will the likely transition from meat to cellular agriculture transform the global food supply chain, shifting how we produce food and what we eat?

KEY MESSAGES

- Cellular agriculture and other no-kill alternatives to farmed meat is likely to be a dramatic disruptor to the global food supply chain.

- Proponents argue that a shift from conventional meat (the industrial meat industry) to alternative products (cellular agriculture and alternative meat) is a powerful climate change mitigation strategy.

- Given the dependence of many nations in the West Pacific on traditional agriculture – the industrial sector and small holders - numerous harmful first and second order implications are possible.

- A country could become a global leader in cellular agriculture if it invests in the science and technology. First and second order impacts could lead to dramatic new food and other downstream technologies.

Signals of Change

Cultured/clean/cell-based meat, now broadly referred to as cellular agriculture, began over two decades ago through NASA funded work (Stephens, 2019). The Dutch Government was instrumental in funding what was then called research into in-vitro meat. Civil society efforts that popularized this approach came in 2008 from PETA (People for the Ethical Treatment of Animals) who offered $1m for the first group to sell in-vitro chicken that could not be distinguished from live-stock chicken. Price parity, a critical factor in moving from niche to mass, and poverty alleviation, is likely within ten years. More concretely:

If renewable energy is used in its production, growing meat directly from cells is likely to compete on costs and have a lower environmental footprint compared to conventional meat production in under 10 years, according to a new pair of studies analysing the life cycle and techno-economics of commercial-scale cultivated meat production (Huling, R., 2021).

Innovation in food, a desire to reduce greenhouse gases i.e., climate change mitigation, the rise of the vegan movement, the fear of zoonosis, and institutional funding have all contributed to invitro meat going from an "impossible" emerging issue to a trend. The current wave of cellular agriculture is led by Silicon Valley Start-ups focused on meat alternatives and 3D printed foods. The next wave is likely to be led by the Asia Pacific Region, as for example with Singapore's approval of cultured meat products (Mischel, 2021). The market for alternative meat (plant-based) is expected to continue to rise in the region, as health fears from traditional meat products rise. Wealth continues to rise as well (Inayatullah and Na, 2018) impacting demand for alternative meat. The Government of the PRC recently invested 300 million in an Israeli based cellular agriculture laboratory (Neo, 2020). Internally, Sun Baoguo, President of the Beijing Technology and Business University argues that:

Cell-based meat analysis are a keyway to guaranteeing China's future meat supply and gaining a leading position when it comes to this production technology will also have an important strategic importance for the country (Neo, 2020).

The drivers of food security, the rise of the vegan movement (meat alternatives, animal welfare), climate change adaptation, COVID-19 and the fear zoonosis, new profits, geo-politics (rising tension in the region) – all suggest that cellular agriculture could go from a niche industry to a dominant wealth producer. While many regions need to make paradigm change to adopt the novel, some do not as alternative meats already exist in their traditions and ecological beliefs.

Depending on the farming sector, the implications generally for traditional farmers and the farming industry are likely to be devastating. Agricultural reliance through the region is varied with Japan at 1% and Australia at 3% and China at 10%. Even though this is low, political parties around agriculture have tremendous lobbying strength especially with food security and safety more and more of an issue.

We summarize how this might play out in the following scenarios.

No Change – Just Hype. In this future, cellular agriculture slowly disappears as it is seen as hype and fake meat, or alternative meat remains niche. Safety concerns become real issues or are overplayed by vested interests in the traditional meat sector. Their recent interest in alternatives because of COVID-19 disappears. As the region gets richer, traditional Western lifestyle diseases spread.

Marginal Change – Joining the Food Chain. In this future, cellular agriculture and alternative meat become niche players in the economy. Consumers see the new meats as inferior products (because of real or political motivated negative health reports) and thus market penetration stalls. Nations invest in the science and technology, citizens groups push these solutions to climate change, and young people become more and more vegan active.

Adaptive Change – Cellular Agriculture is the new Gold. In this future, the new technologies and food choices become dominant by 2040. Consumers shift their food preferences, high paying jobs are created, nations see the benefits to health, zero-net emission pledges are fulfilled, and spin-offs from science and technology food start-ups became a serious source of wealth and health. Wellbeing becomes the regional measurement of success. Lifespans continue to increase. Breakthroughs (from AI and genomics) lead to cellular agriculture becoming the new gold. The traditional meat sector is ravaged by climate change concerns becomes a stranded asset.

Radical Change – Real Home Cooking. In this future, new products emerge from the food revolution including 3D printed cellular agriculture. The home as in the Middle Ages becomes the source of work and food production. Production and consumption are both local and global.

Food Futures
Change Progression Scenarios

FOOD SCENARIOS	NO CHANGE	MARGINAL CHANGE	ADAPTIVE CHANGE	RADICAL CHANGE
NARRATIVE	Just hype	Joining the food chain	The new gold	Real home cooking
STRATEGY	Safety first	Niche market	Scientific breakthrough and market acceptance	3D printed foods for all
KEY SHIFT	Regulation wins out	For the rich	Meat is a stranded asset	Global and local production and consumption

Using the futures method, Causal Layered Analysis (Inayatullah and Milojević, 2015), we summarize this possible shift. Essentially this is a shift from meat as culture to health particular personal health as defining. It is the next industrial revolution.

CLA ON FOOD FUTURES	TODAY	2040
Litany description	Meat challenged by climate change and new demographics.	Shift to protein. Concerns for climate change. Silicon Valley leads the charge.
The system	Food is industrial, managed by large global food corporation with local farmer markets. Negative health implications from life stock meat. Food insecurity.	A new food eco-scape – invitro and alternative meats lead the disruption. The Asia-Pacific region invests and leap-frogs other regions. Reduction in negative health implications of traditional meat. Healthier population. More affordable protein. Enhanced food security and food justice.
The worldview	Agricultural and industrial	Fourth industrial revolution
The myth-metaphor	Meat, today, meat tomorrow, meat forever!	I create my own healthy food!

References and Further Reading

Ho, S. (2019). *The Unstoppable Rise of Veganism*. Green Queen. https://www.greenqueen.com.hk/worldveganday-the-unstoppable-rise-of-veganism/

Inayatullah, S., & Milojević, I. (Eds.). (2015). *CLA 2.0*. Tamsui: Tamkang University.

Inayatullah, S., & Na, L. (2018). *Asia 2038: Ten Disruptions that Change Everything*. Tamsui: Tamkang University. (2020 in Mandarin).

Hunter, E., & Roos, E. (2016). Fear of climate change consequences and predictors of intentions to alter meat consumption. *Food Policy,* 62: 151-160.

Huling, R. (2021). *Groundbreaking New Reports Reveal Massive Environmental Benefits, Cost-Competitiveness of Cultivated Meat*. https://www.gfi-apac.org/blog/groundbreaking-new-reports-reveal-massive-environmental-benefits-cost-competitiveness-of-cultivated-meat/

Lamb, C. (2019). *Cultured Meat Will Likely Debut in Asia, Not Silicon Valley. Here's Why*. https://thespoon.tech/cultured-meat-will-likely-debut-in-asia-not-silicon-valley-heres-why/

Mischel, F. (2021). *Why killing animals for meat could be a thing from the past.* https://synbiobeta.com/does-meat-have-to-come-from-animals-not-anymore/

Neo, P. (2020). *China's cell-based meat future: Calls for national strategy to accelerate sector's growth.* https://www.foodnavigator-asia.com/Article/2020/06/22/China-s-cell-based-meat-future-Calls-for-national-strategy-to-accelerate-sector-s-growth#

Rischer, H., Szilvay, G., & Oskman-Caldentey, K. (2020). Cellular agriculture — industrial biotechnology for food and materials. *Current Opinion in Biotechnology,* 61: 128-134.

Shibata, N., Phoonphongphiphat, A., & Watanabe, S. (2020). *Coronavirus accelerates demand in Asia for plant-based meat.* https://asia.nikkei.com/Business/Food-Beverage/Coronavirus-accelerates-demand-in-Asia-for-plant-based-meat

Stephens, N., Sexton, A., & Driessen, C. (2019, July 10). *Making Sense of Making Meat. Key Moments in the First 20 Years of Tissue Engineering Muscle to Make Food.* Frontiers in Sustainable Food Systems. https://www.frontiersin.org/articles/10.3389/fsufs.2019.00045/full

Rubio, N., Xiang, N., & Kaplan, D. (2020). Plant-based and cell-based approaches to meat production. *Nature Communications,* (11) No. 6276. https://www.nature.com/articles/s41467-020-20061-y

Wolf, M. (2021, March 9). *Here's what needs to happen for cultivated meat to hit price parity in 5 years.* https://thespoon.tech/heres-what-needs-to-happen-for-cultivated-meat-to-hit-price-parity-in-5-years/

Women Really Lead the Way: the pendulum swings

Women Really Lead the Way: which future for gender equity, shattered dreams or transition toward a partnership society?

KEY MESSAGES

- COVID-19 has reversed previous gains related to gender and socio-economic equity.

- Long standing policy drivers such as closing of the gender gaps in education, health as well as economy and politics are mitigating this reversal.

- Based on the emerging issues, two futures scenarios are possible from here and to 2050: (1) The Continuation of the Shattered Dreams and Hopes for the Future and (2) The Pendulum Swings – the latter being in alignment with the 'gender equity as the desired future' vision.

Signals of Change

In our 2018 book Asia 2038: Ten Disruptions That Change Everything (Inayatullah and Na, 2018) we asserted that the rise of women and gender equity is major and foundational shift, a critical disruption. The key driver of the change has been an increase in women's economic and political power, i.e., there has been an increasing number of women entrepreneurs on executive and legislative boards and in politics and business. Another driver includes a drop in birth rates influencing women moving out of the private sphere into the public sphere. A third significant driver – a pull of the future – is that gender equity is increasingly and explicitly becoming an image of a desired future.

We also stressed that, even though we investigated relatively weak yet potentially powerful signals of change, it is important to note that the future is uncertain. Because of that, it is important to regularly revisit early signals of change, in light of new circumstances. Arguably, the most critical factor impacting not only the Asia-Pacific but the world since 2019 has been the COVID-19 Pandemic. Due to the pandemic, the region is undergoing yet another major and foundational shift. The text that follows overviews the current situation and future projections/current trends as they relate to the inclusion of women. We then investigate other possibilities for the future, based on emerging issues and weak signals. The findings are organised within two scenarios, the "Shattered Dreams and Hopes for the Future" and "The Pendulum Swings".

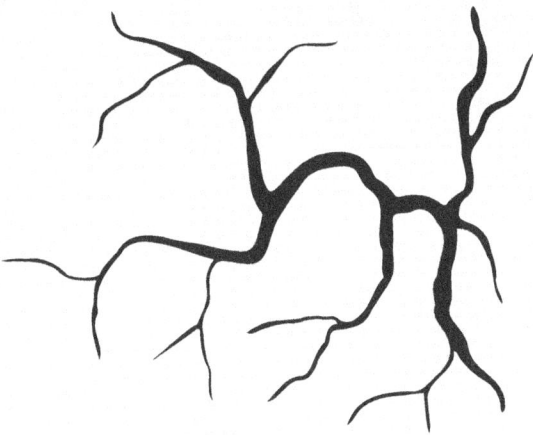

Shattered Dreams and Hopes for the Future

The COVID-19 Pandemic has, so far, amplified gender disparities. The gains made over the past several decades towards the inclusion of women have been eroded and practices rooted in gender inequality and patriarchal structures have resurfaced. For example, child marriage, known to significantly increase the likelihood of poverty, violence and ill-health for women and their families, has increased in some areas. Tens of thousands of young girls have already been impacted. It is currently estimated that nearly 200,000 more girls are at risk of child marriage in 2020 in South Asia (Save the Children, 2020a). Globally, at current rates, a further 2.5 million girls are at risk of early marriage by 2025 because of the pandemic (Save the Children, 2020b) and 150 million more girls might be married as children by 2030 (Girls Not Brides, 2021). Indeed, the "Covid generation [is likely] to be robbed of a fair chance in life" (Mashriq TV, 2021) because of an increase in human trafficking and the difficulty of rescuing survivors of human trafficking due to border closures (Blue Dragon, 2021; Neal, 2020). Further, negatively impacting the future inclusion of women is the massive drop out from formal education – currently impacting millions of girls. It is estimated that twenty percent of girls in East Asia and the Pacific, or close to 40 million in total, have not been able to access distance learning during the pandemic, whilst nearly 69 percent reported studying and learning less than usual (Babb and Buchanan, 2020). In South and West Asia, "2.8 million women and girls may not be able to return to education, from pre-primary to tertiary levels" (Babb and Buchanan, 2020).

Domestic and gender-based violence is on the increase – it is estimated that for every additional three months of lockdown 15 million additional cases of gender-based violence worldview is likely (UNESCAP 2020). Countries such as Singapore, Malaysia, Fiji, and Samoa, have all reported increases in call volumes to domestic violence helplines – in a range from 33 per cent to doubling (UNESCAP, 2020). Domestic violence has soared everywhere, including in countries such as Australia and New Zealand (Kennedy, 2020; Leask, 2020). In countries with the tradition of female genital mutilation, the progress towards ending it by 2030 is severely challenged due to pandemic-related disruptions in prevention programmes (UNFPA, 2020). As a result, 2 million FGM cases could occur over the next decade that would otherwise have been averted (UNFPA, 2020). Other gender-based disparities negatively impacting women – e.g., the digital divide, income inequality, wage loss and unemployment, limited access to healthcare and other important services, unpaid care work, deterioration of mental health and gender stereotyping – have all been exacerbated because of COVID-19 (Asia Pacific Forum, 2020; Zhuang, 2020). These factors are cumulative suggesting that the Shattered Dreams and Hopes for the Future scenario will continue and previous gains from the inclusion of women may all but disappear.

The Pendulum Swings

COVID-19 provides us with an opportunity for radical, positive action to redress long-standing inequalities in multiple areas of women's lives. There is scope for not just endurance, but recovery and growth. (Mlambo-Ngcuka, 2020)

At the same time, it is precisely these gains from the past that are opening up avenues for initiatives which aim to not only address the worsening inequality as a result of the pandemic but also historical patterns of power distribution between genders. Countless local, national, regional and international organisations have made a commitment to "scale up their activities in response to the new challenges created by the COVID-19 pandemic" (UN Women, 2020: 18). They have recognised that a strong post-pandemic recovery also requires gender-responsive measures (ILO, 2020). With the recognition that, globally, women make up 70 per cent of frontline workers in the health and social sector (Mlambo-Ngcuka, 2020), demands for women's equal representation in all COVID-19 response planning and decision-making – including in the senior positions in the global health workforce – are increasingly heard (Investing in Women, 2021, Guatteres, 2020). Indeed, numerous NGOs, local banks as well as the World Bank and the Asian Development Bank are already implementing projects hoping to "empower women and build capacity" (Nanthini and Nair, 2020). These projects aim at protecting "women from discrimination, horrid working conditions and unfair wages, and an over-burden of care more than their participation in decision-making and the prevention of structural violence inflicted upon them" (Nanthini and Nair, 2020). All these issues are long-standing patterns of power distribution between genders – the pandemic has made the issue of addressing them even more urgent.

Global organisations and research institutes are increasingly putting a 'price tag' on the lack of women's inclusion, that is, they are taking note of the serious financial gains to be made from the inclusion of women. This issue will thus become increasingly important in the post-pandemic economic and social recovery.

In 2018 McKinsey Global Institute estimated that "advancing women's equality in the countries of Asia Pacific could add $4.5 trillion to their collective annual GDP in 2025, a 12 percent increase over the business-as-usual trajectory" (MacKinsey & Co, 2018). The International Labour Organisation made similar warnings ten years ago – the overall cost of gender inequality in Asia alone was estimated at $US 47 billion per year. By not addressing the gender gap in the workforce, countries around the world stand to lose a potential boost to global employment by tens of millions of workers and most of these gains are said to be in emerging economies like those in Southeast Asia (ILO, 2017).

Gender equality, then, "is a business imperative" (Nanthini and Nair, 2020). The inclusion of women as the business imperative will become even more critical as we move into the future: "attempts to incorporate more women into the workforce ... will be absolutely necessary to 'ride out' the economic downturn post-pandemic" (Nanthini and Nair, 2020).

While these numbers may sound 'abstract' – not in the here and now - to some, the widely reported story of BioNTech co-founder Dr Özlem Türeci in producing a new technology and one of the first COVID-19 vaccines (The Pfizer/BioNTech), has brought the issue of gender equality further into the spotlight. It was the company's gender balanced workforce, Türeci said, that helped accelerate the development of the vaccine (The Guardian, 2021). "At BioNTech", she specified, "women make up 54% of our total workforce and 45% of top management ... a gender-balanced team has been critical to making the seemingly impossible possible – developing a Covid-19 vaccine within 11 months without shortcuts." A similar story has been reported by one of the developers of the Oxford/AstraZeneca vaccine Professor Sarah Gilbert: "On the vaccine team in Oxford, two-thirds are female, and all have worked incredibly hard for over a year, often while dealing with family responsibilities" (The Guardian, 2021). Both scientists, however, raised an issue of unequal distribution of top positions which destroys the opportunity of mobilising precious talent, destroying value not only for stakeholders but also costing our societies and our futures.

Still, while the COVID-19 crisis has unveiled and amplified gender disparities, it has also shone light on the strengths of female leadership. Two years into the pandemic, an often quoted 'success story' in managing the pandemic is the leadership of New Zealand's Prime Minister Jacinta Ardern. Her leadership style – focused on empathy plus expertise – is increasingly recognised as the way to the future, not only for the Asia-Pacific, but the world as a whole. The leadership of Jacinta Ardern and many other women has been increasingly recognised by both national bodies and international organisations (UN WOMEN, 2020a; 2020b; 2021). Further to this, many national governments have provided measures which helped avoid the worst effects from the pandemic. Some of those measures – even though not sufficient and fully adequate – have been aimed at supporting women. Another positive development has been the enhancement of the regional cooperation – this cooperation "has been robust across multiple sectors" (Guterres, 2020).

Multi organisational alliances are also taking place, for example, as safe houses in Malaysia and Indonesia reached full capacity, there was a focus on alternative solution such as the rent of temporary rooms and the formalisation of multi organisational guidelines (Sambhi, 2020). Online and mobile service providers took steps to deliver support such as free calls to helplines and provision of online resources aimed at breaking the silence and exposing gender-based violence (UN Women, 2020a). These innovative virtual solutions include in China #AntiDomesticViolenceDuringEpidemic, or an online text chat service for women in distress unable to call the helpline and speak over the phone in Singapore. United Nations Economic and Social Commission reports similar initiatives and measures taken across Asia-Pacific to combat violence against women (UN ESCAP, 2020). A policy paper by UN Women (2020a) lists many similar examples of measures taken in countries such as Brunei Darussalam, Fiji, and Tonga.

In conclusion, women's strengths, and the seeds of change towards gender equity, as summarised in, for example, the UN Women Asia and the Pacific Annual Report published in 2018 and in Inayatullah and Na (2018) are still current and relevant.

These strengths, coupled with 'gender equity as the desired future', have only reinforced the resolve to remove various obstacle preventing women's inclusion. We can thus anticipate that such momentum – The Pendulum Swing – will continue well into the future.

References and Further Reading

Asia Pacific Forum (2020). *The Impact of COVID-19 on Women and Girls,* https://www.asiapacificforum.net/media/resource_file/Women__Girls_COVID19_Impact_Snapshot.pdf

AWARE (2020). *Women's Care Centre: Call-back and Chat Service,* 2020. https://www.aware.org.sg/womens-care -centre/callback-chat/

Azcona, G., Bhatt, A., Davies, S.E., Harman S., Smith J., & Wenham, C. (2020). *Spotlight on Gender, COVID-19 and the SDGs: Will the Pandemic Derail Hard-Won Progress on Gender Equality?* UN Women, New York. https://www.unwomen.org/-/media/headquarters/attachments/sections/library/publications/2020/spotlight-on-gender-covid-19-and-the-sdgs-en.pdf?la=en&vs=5013

Babb, J., & Buchanan, N. (2020). *COVID-19 Leaves Millions of Girls at Risk of School Dropout in Asia-Pacific.* The Diplomat. https://thediplomat.com/2020/11/covid-19-leaves-millions-of-girls-at-risk-of-school-dropout-in-asia-pacific/

Blue Dragon (2021). https://www.bluedragon.org/

Girls Not Brides (2021). https://www.girlsnotbrides.org/

The Guardian (2021). *BioNTech Co-founder Says Gender Equality Made Vaccine Possible.* https://www.theguardian.com/world/2021/mar/08/biontech-co-founder-says-gender-equality-made-vaccine-possible

Guetteres, A. (2020). *Target Women in all Aspects of Economic Recovery and Stimulus Plans in Southeast Asia.* https://www.un.org/en/coronavirus/target-women-all-aspects-economic-recovery-and-stimulus-plans-southeast-asia

ILO (2020). *Gendered Impacts of COVID-19 on the Garment Sector, International Labour Organization.* http://www.ilo.org/wcmsp5/groups/public/---asia/---ro-bangkok/---sro-bangkok/documents/publication/wcms_760374.pdf

ILO (2017). *World Employment Social Outlook.* https://www.ilo.org/wcmsp5/groups/public/---dgreports/---dcomm/---publ/documents/publication/wcms_541211.pdf

Inayatullah, S. & Na, L. (2018). *Asia 2038: Ten Disruptions That Change Everything.* Tamkang University Press, Taipei.

Investing in Women (2021) . *The Case for Workplace Gender Equality.*
https://investinginwomen.asia/

Kennedy, E. (2020). *'The Worst Year': Domestic Violence Soars in Australia During COVID-19.* The Guardian,
https://www.theguardian.com/society/2020/dec/01/the-worst-year-domestic-violence-soars-in-australia-during-covid-19

Leask, A. (2020). *Domestic Violence Increases Rapidly in New Zealand - Strangulation, Beatings 'Commonplace' in 2020.* New Zealand Herald,
https://www.nzherald.co.nz/nz/domestic-violence-increases-rapidly-in-new-zealand-strangulation-beatings-commonplace-in-2020/TKNYCLLUVQMBANS4QNXFXORLLM/

MacKinsey & Co (2018). *The Power of Parity: Advancing Women's Equality in Asia Pacific.* https://www.mckinsey.com/featured-insights/gender-equality/the-power-of-parity-advancing-womens-equality-in-asia-pacific#

Mashriq TV (2021). *Virus Despair Forces Girls Across Asia Into Child Marriage.*
https://mashriqtv.pk/latest/60065

Mlambo-Ngcuka, P. (2020). *COVID-19: Women Front and Centre.*
https://www.unwomen.org/en/news/stories/2020/3/statement-ed-phumzile-covid-19-women-front-and-centre

Nanthini, S., & Nair, T. (2020.) *COVID-19 and the Impacts on Women.* NTS Insight, No. IN20-05, Singapore: RSIS Centre for Non-Traditional Security Studies, Nanyang Technological University,
https://reliefweb.int/sites/reliefweb.int/files/resources/NTS-Insight_COVID-19-and-the-Impacts-on-Women-30July2020.pdf

Neal, W. (2020). *Corona Stalls Rescue of Vietnam's Trafficked Brides, OCCRP: Organized Crime and Corruption Reporting Project.*
https://www.occrp.org/en/daily/11850-corona-stalls-rescue-of-vietnam-s-trafficked-brides

Sambhi, S. (2020). *COVID-19 and the Increase in Domestic Violence in Asia Pacific.* https://www.eco-business.com/news/covid-19-and-the-increase-in-domestic-violence-in-asia-pacific/

Save the Children (2020a). *COVID-19 Places Half A Million More Girls at Risk of Child Marriage In 2020.* https://www.savethechildren.net/news/covid-19-places-half-million-more-girls-risk-child-marriage-2020

Save the Children (2020b). *COVID-19 Causing Greatest Surge of Child Marriages in 25 Years.* https://www.savethechildren.org.au/media/media-releases/covid-19-causing-greatest-surge-of-child-marriages

UN ESCAP (2020). *The COVID-19 Pandemic and Violence Against Women in Asia and the Pacific.* United Nations Economic and Social Commission for Asia and the Pacific. https://www.unescap.org/sites/default/files/20201119_SDD_Policy_Paper_Covid-19.pdf

UN Women (2018). *Annual Report: Asia and the Pacific 2017-2018.* https://www2.unwomen.org/-/media/field%20office%20eseasia/docs/publications/2019/06/unw_annual-report-2018-r12.pdf?la=en&vs=1341

UN Women (2020a). *Policy Brief: The Impact of COVID-19 on Women.* https://asiapacific.unwomen.org/en/digital-library/publications/2020/04/policy-brief-the-impact-of-covid-19-on-women

UN Women (2020b). *Five Women on the Front Lines of COVID Response.* https://www.unwomen.org/en/news/stories/2020/4/compilation-women-on-the-front-lines-of-covid-response

UN WOMEN (2021). *This is What Leadership Looks Like: Meet Jittirat Tantasirin, Creating Opportunities for Women in the Automotive Industry in Thailand.* https://asiapacific.unwomen.org/en/news-and-events/stories/2021/03/what-leadership-looks-like-jittirat-tantasirin

UNFPA (2020). *Impact of the COVID-19 Pandemic on Family Planning and Ending Gender-based Violence, Female Genital Mutilation and Child Marriage, Interim Technical Note.* https://www.unfpa.org/sites/default/files/resource-pdf/COVID-19_impact_brief_for_UNFPA_24_April_2020_1.pdf

Zhuang, C. (2020). *Impacts of COVID-10 on Women in the Asia-Pacific Region.* https://www.fawco.org/un-advocacy/gender-equality/commission-on-the-status-of-women/csw-blogs/4469-impacts-of-covid-19-on-women-and-girls-in-the-asia-pacific-region

The Changing Family: robots as carers and other transformations

The Changing Family: will the family, stable for generations, if not hundreds of years, transform, becoming more diversified and inclusive of social and technological changes?

KEY MESSAGES

- Traditional family forms – whether extended or nuclear – are undergoing significant change.

- The definition of the family, and who and what is included, is likely to continue to diversify as who constitutes a family member changes.

- The drivers of these changes include the advent of new disruptive technologies, changing social values, rise of the women's movements, and long term structural economic changes challenging the normalization of women's unpaid labour in the household.

- The future gap in care – as family members increasingly are unlikely to provide unpaid care – will increase efforts to outsource care to technology and paid health care workers.

- Insofar as health policies and systems are based on certain assumptions about the family's role in the provision of health care, as the family changes so will health futures.

Signals of Change

As we consider the changes ahead, there are several weak signals that suggest that the emerging issue of the changing nature of the family will be a significant disrupter to social futures. These weak signals include:

- New technologies, social robots and AI are already being used in the care of elderly, sick and disabled.

- Fewer family members to assist with unpaid caring and the rise of paid long-term services.

- The decreased use of palliative and end of life care and the increased use of euthanasia and assisted suicide.

- The rise of sex trained therapists – human and robot – for persons with disability.

- The normalization of gay/lesbian marriages.

- The beginnings of robot/AI human marriages.

Disruptions Ahead

In many parts of the world, the family has remained stable over generations with clear roles assigned to family members and a clear definition of the family. Whether traditional families are extended and intergenerational or nuclear, they have been a foundational unit upon which health policies and systems are based. Families are expected to provide the bulk of care for their young, old and ill members. Without this assumption the current health systems would cease to adequately function. But what might happen if these family forms are disrupted?

Already, in some parts of the world, the extended family has all but disappeared. In others, it is increasingly under threat – due to urbanisation, the availability of work (or the lack of), globalisation, migration, industrialisation, and automation. In many cases, family members who previously provided unpaid health care are no longer able to (because of inter-state or international migration, for example). Another significant factor which has impacting the provision of health care is the "Silver Tsunami" – the demographic trend of a globally aging population requiring a higher quantity and quality of care.

Apart from these economic, demographic, and cultural changes, the form the family is increasingly taking is likely to shift; for example, there is a move away from arranged and toward love marriages in certain societies. And, as more and more women become educated and financially independent, they tend to marry later and have fewer children. The percentage of single, unmarried women in their 30s and 40s – previously unheard of in some societies – has been steadily increasing (Inayatullah and Na, 2018: 22). The increasing rate of divorce also impacts on the type of family – creating single parent or blended families.

Moreover, the LGBTQ movement and the legalisation of same-sex marriages impacts family norms as well. Assisted reproduction technologies have also changed traditional definitions of the biological family (through donor eggs and sperm, for example). Their future developments will likely have further impact especially with the creation of the artificial womb (BBC, 2019). Finally, the normalization of relations with AI/Robots (Inayatullah, 2020; Chou, 2012) will significantly alter the nature of the future family, and its implications for public health.

Further Diversification

We can thus expect that going towards 2050, traditional extended and nuclear biological families will become further diversified. To start with new technologies, social robots and AI have already found their use in the care of elderly, sick and disabled. These include E—health (i.e., Telehealth, Telecare, Telemedicine, Tele-coaching, and Mobile Health). Daily life supportive assistive technologies and robotic technology are found to be of significant use for people who cannot rely on friends and family (Hill-Cawthorne et al, 2019, Swain, 2020). We can reasonably expect that technological innovations will continue to be developed, most likely exponentially. Further to this, with 'the age of pandemics' potentially upon us, individuals craving physical contact and struggling with loneliness will increase and so will demand for novel health care.

However, many technological innovations rely on a set of assumption regarding who constitutes a family. That is, most of the devices are designed to support unpaid caregivers (i.e., family members who constitute most caregivers) (Lindeman, 2020). For example, virtual reality headsets offering simulation in which family caregivers take on the persona of their family member facing a variety of situations (e.g., with Alzheimer's or Parkinson's disease) assume the existence of family caregivers wishing to develop more empathy for those in their care and improve the way the care is delivered (Halpert, 2019; Swain, 2020). But if the current trends towards reduction and fragmentation of the family continue, where will these family members be found? Who will they be?

Another weak signal is the increase in human and robot/AI "marriages". While no state currently recognises such marriages legally for those that partake the relationship is felt as very real (Inayatullah and Na, 2018). A technological driver behind these changes includes new technological advancements in AI that are normalizing robots and robots increasingly becoming more sophisticated and looking like humans. Other drivers include changes in demography and culture – e.g., fewer females being available because of child selection methods preferring males in some societies. Finally, the rise in loneliness globally has seen people bonding with their techno-pets – extending the family via robot pets in the home. This is likely to continue as research shows positive effect of both real and robot dogs and cats on human brain chemistry and some beneficial health effects, like lowering blood pressure and boosting the i mmune system (Inayatullah and Na, 2018; Pirhonen et al, 2020; Gustafsson, 2015).

Yet another weak signal is the normalisation of gay/lesbian or same-sex marriages. Debates over same-sex marriage are increasingly heard yet they remain a controversial social and political issue. This has significant implications on health care – i.e., where homosexuality is pathologized medical 'cures' are still offered (i.e., gay conversion or electroshock therapies) and same-sex partners are commonly prevented or not consulted in relation to providing the auxiliary health care. If the norm shifts – towards normalisation and acceptance of the same-sex marriages – the assumptions as to who is to formally provide health care will also change.

The fourth weak signal is related to the outsourcing of specific types of health care and support to paid professionals which were traditionally provided by family members. There is a lack of adequate data in terms of how much of the health care is provided by family members and how much by paid professionals (IACO, 2021; WHO, 2006). Current estimates of the economic value of unpaid care for EU Member States ranges from 50% to 90% of the overall cost of the formal long-term care provision (Merck KgaA, 2017). In the US, estimates are between 45 and 65.7 million unpaid family caregivers who are providing care to someone who is ill, disabled, or aged – compared to 5 million paid caregivers (Merck KgaA, 2017; Lindeman et al, 2020). The figures for UK and Australia are 6.5 million and 2,7 million unpaid caregivers, respectively (Merck KgaA, 2017; AIHW, 2019). 100 million caregivers in Europe consist of 20% of the EU population (Merck KgaA, 2017). Globally, most unpaid family caregivers are women, the estimates range anywhere between 70% and 90% (Armstrong, 2013; UNESCAP, 2019; Boniol, 2019; WHO, 2013; WHO, 2019). But as unpaid family carers are no longer able or unwilling to provide this care, the social and economic pressure exponentially rises for governments to provide additional funding. The cost of this funding will be staggering – an estimate of an economic cost to replace all informal care in Australia alone for 2020 is 77.9% billion (Deloitte, 2020). The demand will be compounded by the growth in the population of older people in need of care and by the expectations of what constitutes quality care. Adequate data – trend extrapolations of this growth – for most countries is also missing. Indicative is the estimate for the US population: "by 2050, the number of individuals using paid long-term services in any setting (e.g., at home, residential care such as assisted living, or skilled nursing facilities) will likely double from the 13 million using services in 2000, to 27 million people" (FCA, 2021). Many of those individuals will be women in need of rather than as providers of care.

As longevity increases, another weak signal suggests the decreased use of palliative and end of life care and the increased use of euthanasia and assisted suicide.

Various technological devices (such as The Deliverance Machine, Thanatron and Mercitron) have already been used for voluntary euthanasia or assisted suicide and the trend is likely to accelerate. A "futuristic suicide machine" Sarco is currently in development with the goal of becoming widely available through the open-source 3D printing technology (Shinkman, 2019; Exit International, 2021).

Further to these economic and demographic drivers, a different set of expectations as to what constitutes quality care are emerging. Under "future directions" WHO has already identified the move towards "more pro-equity, efficient, decentralized and people-centred services" in the Western Pacific (WHO 2018). For example, few people would currently oppose making the public realm of space, social services and jobs accessible to women and men with disabilities, argue Kulick & Rydström (2015), and proceed with asking the following: "But what about access to the private realm of desire and sexuality? How can one also facilitate access to that, in ways that respect the integrity of disabled adults, and also of those people who work with and care for them?"

This issue has recently come to the fore in the highly publicised case in Australia when the Administrative Appeals Tribunal granted a woman with multiple sclerosis the right to have a sex therapist paid for under the National Disability Insurance Scheme (NDIS) (Yau, 2019). In 2020, after Federal Government challenges this decision, the Federal Court upheld it and ruled that the use of a specially trained sex therapist was both "reasonable and necessary" support to be funded under the Scheme (Skatssoon, J. 2020, Dickinson and Smith, 2020, Henrique-Gomes, 2020). Inability to form a family/partnership has been cited as a key factor as to why the woman in question would require outsourcing intimacy to the paid worker. While these issues may not be part of a current discussion in other parts of the world, we could expect that they may become so in the future.

This is because, for disability advocates, sexual services are a type of mental and physical health therapy critical for fulfilling basic human needs for "intimacy, validation, stress relief and stronger self-esteem" (Ward, 2014). Sex therapy is thus framed as both a human rights and health issue without which a person with a disability is "effectively denied the right to sexual health, pleasure and well-being" (Dickinson and Smith, 2020). More and more novel issues are likely to result as the nature of health rights, disruptive technologies, ageing, and challenges to unpaid work continue.

Conclusion: Four Areas of Change (at Least)

To conclude, there are numerous trends and weak signals suggesting that the future will see changing forms of the family and the impact of this change on the future of health and health systems. Several sets of changes may take place.

First, there could be far fewer marriages overall, as females marry less and participate in the formal economy more – a trend across many parts of the world. This will impact the size of the family, and who will be available to provide care. Continuation of the trends regarding the ageing population will also change some underlying assumption in regard to health care.

Second, as seen by the previous examples, the new families could include ones with AI forms, such as robots in Japan, China, and Republic of Korea. It is to be expected that many health services – including those currently provided by the unpaid family carers – will be further outsourced through novel technological innovations.

Third, new types of family that include lesbian, gay, bi-sexual, and transgender individuals are also emerging and have already been normalised in countries such as Australia and New Zealand.

Finally, there is a different set of expectations as to what constitutes quality care and who will provide that care.

In a nutshell, as the form of the family changes, traditional arrangements underpinning health care will also change. The norm of what/who constitutes the family and who can/will provide health care will continue to shift.

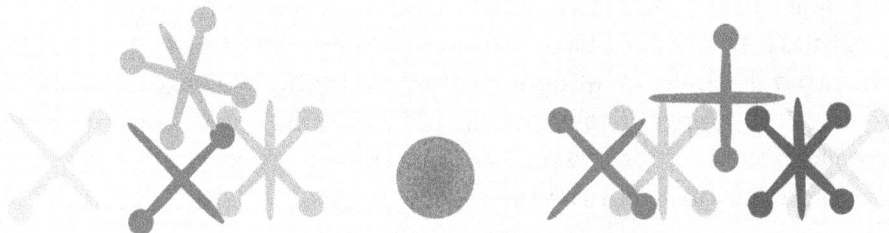

References and Further Reading

AIHW (2019). *Informal Carers. Australian Government, Australian Institute of Health and Welfare.* https://www.aihw.gov.au/reports/australias-welfare/informal-carers

Armstrong, P. (2013). *Unpaid Health Care: An Indicator of Equity. Pan American Health Organization, Office of Gender, Diversity and Human Rights.* https://www.paho.org/hq/dmdocuments/2013/Unpaid-health-care-indicator-equity-Pat-Armstrong-2013.pdf

BBC (2019, October 16). *The World's First Artificial Womb for Humans.* https://www.bbc.com/news/av/health-50056405

Boniol, M., McIsaac, M., Xu, L., Wuliji, T., Diallo, K., & Campbell, J. (2019). *Gender Equity in the Health Workforce: Analysis of 104 Countries.* https://apps.who.int/iris/bitstream/handle/10665/311314/WHO-HIS-HWF-Gender-WP1-2019.1-eng.pdf?sequence=1&isAllowed=y

Chou, Y. (2012). The Changing Social Meanings of Pets and their Alternative Futures. *Journal of Futures Studies,* 17(2): 1-14.

Convention on the Rights of Persons with Disabilities (2006). *UN department of Economic and Social Affairs.* https://www.un.org/development/desa/disabilities/convention-on-the-rights-of-persons-with-disabilities.html#Fulltext

Deloitte (2020). *The Value of Informal Care in 2020. Carers Australia.* Deloitte Access Economics. https://apo.org.au/sites/default/files/resource-files/2020-07/apo-nid307225.pdf

Dickinson, H., & Smith, C. (2020). *Why It Is 'Reasonable and Necessary' for the NDIS to Support People's Sex Lives.* University of New South Wales Newsroom. https://newsroom.unsw.edu.au/news/social-affairs/why-it-reasonable-and-necessary-ndis-support-peoples-sex-lives

Exit International (2021). *Sarco. (Re)design death.* https://www.exitinternational.net/sarco/

FCA (2021). *Selected Long-Term Care Statistics.* Family Caregiver Alliance (FCA). https://www.caregiver.org/resource/selected-long-term-care-statistics/

Gustafsson, C., Syanberg, C., & Müllersdorf, M. (2015). Using a Robotic Cat in Dementia Care: A Pilot Study. *Journal of Gerontological Nursing,* 41(10): 45-56.

FCA (2021). *Selected Long-Term Care Statistics*. Family Caregiver Alliance (FCA). https://www.caregiver.org/resource/selected-long-term-care-statistics/

Gustafsson, C., Syanberg, C., & Müllersdorf, M. (2015). Using a Robotic Cat in Dementia Care: A Pilot Study. *Journal of Gerontological Nursing, 41*(10): 45-56.

Halper, J. (2019). *7 New Tech Devices for Elder Care That Help Seniors Live Happier, Healthier Lives*. CNBC. https://www.cnbc.com/2019/09/12/7-new-tech-devices-for-that-help-seniors-live-happier-healthier-lives.html

Henriques-Gomes, L. (2020). *NDIS Funds May Be Used to Pay For Sex Workers, Court Rules*. The Guardian. https://www.theguardian.com/australia-news/2020/may/12/ndis-funds-pay-sex-workers-court-rules

Hill-Cawthorne, G., Limén, H., Niezen, M., & Tennøe, T. (2019). *Technologies in Care for Older People. European Parliamentary Technology Assessment (EPTA) report*. The Swedish Parliament: Stockholm. https://eptanetwork.org/images/documents/minutes/EPTA_report_2019.pdf

IACO (2021). *Global Carer Facts*. International Alliance of Carer Organizations. https://internationalcarers.org/carer-facts/global-carer-stats/

Inayatullah, S. (2020, January 18). *Will You Marry Robots and Other Disruptions Changing the Futures of Asia*. Futures Platform. https://www.futuresplatform.com/blog/will-you-marry-robots-and-other-disruptions-changing-futures-asia

Inayatullah, S., & Na, L. (2018). *Asia 2038: Ten Disruptions That Change Everything*. Taipei: Tamkang University Press.

Kulick, D., & Rydström, J. (2015). *Loneliness and Its Opposite: Sex, Disability, and the Ethics of Engagement*. Durham, NC: Duke University Press.

Lindeman, D.A., Kim, K.K., Gladstone, C., & Apesoa-Varano, E.C. (2020). Technology and Caregiving: Emerging Interventions and Directions for Research. *The Gerontologist, 60*(1), S41–S49.

Merck KGaA (2017). *Embracing the Critical Role of Caregivers Around the World. White Paper and Action Plan*. https://www.embracingcarers.com/content/dam/web/healthcare/corporate/embracing-carers/media/infographics /us/Merck%20KGaA%20Embracing%20Carers_White%20Paper%20Flattened.pdf

Pirhonen, J., Tiilikainen, E., Pekkarinen, S., Lemivaara, M., & Melkas, H. (2020). Can Robots Tackle Late-Life Loneliness? Scanning of Future Opportunities and Challenges In Assisted Living Facilities. Futures, 124 (December), 102640.

Shinkman, R. (2019). A Futuristic Suicide Machine Aims to End the Stigma of Assisted Dying. Leaps.org. https://leaps.org/a-futuristic-suicide-machine-aims-to-end-the-stigma-of-assisted-dying/particle-1

Skatssoon, J. (2020). Court Rules NDIS Can Fund Sex Workers. Government News. https://www.governmentnews.com.au/court-rules-ndis-must-fund-sex-workers/

Swain, F. (2020). *The Technologies That Could Transform Ageing.* BBC. https://www.bbc.com/future/article/20201104-the-technologies-that-could-transform-ageing

Tøssebro, J. (2016). Scandinavian Disability Policy: From Deinstitutionalisation to Non-Discrimination and Beyond. *Alter,* 10 (2):111-123.

UNESCAP (2019). *Unpaid Work in Asia and the Pacific. Social Development Policy Papers, 2019/02.* United Nationals Economic and Social Commission for Asia and the Pacific. https://www.unescap.org/sites/default/files/PP_2019-02_Unpaid%20Work.pdf

Ward, M. (2014). *The Surprising Way the Netherlands Is Helping Its Disabled Have Sex.* Mic. https://www.mic.com/articles/85201/the-surprising-way-the-netherlands-is-helping-its-disabled-have-sex

WHO (2006). *Health Workers: A Global Profile.* The World Health Report. https://www.who.int/whr/2006/06_chap1_en.pdf

WHO (2013). *Understanding Health Labour Markets in the Western Pacific Region.* World Health Organization. https://www.who.int/publications/i/item/understanding-health-labor-markets-in-the-western-pacific-region

WHO (2018). *Primary Health Care in The Western Pacific Region – Looking Back And Future Directions.* World Health Organization, Western Pacific Region. https://www.who.int/docs/default-source/primary-health-care-conference/phc-regional-report-western-pacific.pdf?sfvrsn=5fbff145_2

WHO (2019). *Delivered by Women, Led by Men: A Gender and Equity Analysis of the Global Health and Social Workforce.* https://www.who.int/hrh/resources/en_exec-summ_delivered-by-women-led-by-men.pdf?ua=1

Yau, M. (2019). *Finally, the NDIS Will Fund Sex Therapy. But It Should Cover Sex Workers Too.* SBS News. https://www.sbs.com.au/news/finally-the-ndis-will-fund-sex-therapy-but-it-should-cover-sex-workers-too

Learning Anytime, Anywhere, with Anyone: emerging pedagogical futures

Learning Anytime, Anywhere, With Anyone: will learning transform, moving from the factory model to alternative paradigms such as the ecological or the digital?

KEY MESSAGES

- A shift away from the factory model of education to a facilitative model of learning is currently taking place.

- A shift toward models that are student and choice centered are emerging.

- A shift toward hybrid and metaverse models of teaching and learning.

- Nations and economies that shift to this model sooner will have the competitive advantage in the future.

- The shift is led by digital natives.

- Fluidity, adaptability, and relevance are their core expectations as in the uberification of education models.

- Businesses are leading in this area. This is likely to pressure universities and schools to adopt pedagogies that are more market-relevant, that lead to skills and competencies that they require.

- The COVID-19 pandemic is enhancing trends towards e-learning but reversing gains in relation to gender and socio-economic equity.

Signals of Change

The new emergent world of teaching and learning is drastically shifting traditional approaches of education. To summarise, the old approach to education was based on 'the factory model'. Classes and curriculum were time and space standardised. Vocational and technically measurable aspects of education, focused on the production of quantifiable and narrowly useful outcomes were dominant (Milojević, 2003). The educational system was hierarchical – with the ministry and the principal at the top, followed by teachers then students. The complete educational experience was highly structured, primarily based on age-based cohorts rather than the interests and abilities of students. There was one directional communication. First, students were given facts and truths as defined by the teachers, curriculum, and ministries of education. Second, students regurgitated those facts and truths. The keys to success were discipline, obedience, and the ability to memorise and recite. The reward for reciting the truth as defined by the curriculum was an accreditation, which was then used for employment.

While this traditional approach remains active in many parts of the world, it is been eroded and will continue to transform in the next twenty years. This is occurring for a number of reasons: the advent of new technologies, demand from digital natives, and, of course, COVID-19 has significantly changed how we learn. The factory model even when used has lost legitimacy. Neither educators nor policy planners anticipate that such approach will strengthen in the future, rather, it is expected to weaken even further to the point of almost completely disappearing in the coming decades.

Drivers

There are several drivers of this shift. The COVID-19 pandemic has accelerated some of the shifts and slowed down, even reversed the others. For example, prior to the pandemic, the number of students enrolled in higher education was expected to double to 262 million by 2025, with most the growth in nations such as India and China; over eight million of these students were anticipated to travel to other countries (Inayatullah, 2020b). The market size for global education was 2.5 trillion dollars in 2011; it grew to 4.4 trillion US dollars by 2017. In the same period, the e-learning was projected to grow by 25% (Inayatullah, 2020b). Due to border closures the travel to other countries has all but seized. Australian universities alone have lost more than 17,000 jobs with further cuts likely (Zhou, 2021). While the decade from 2009 to 2018 saw Australian universities enjoy an unprecedented boom in international student enrolments – the revenue from this activity increase by 260%, from AUD$3.4 billion to AUD$8.8 billion (Marshman & Larkins, 2021) – the sector lost 1.8 billion in 2020 and is projected to lose a further 2 billion in 2021. Modelling by Universities Australia shows the sector will lose A$16 billion by 2023 and AUD $18 billion by 2024 (Zhou, 2021, Marshman & Larkins, 2021). E-learning, on the other hand, has skyrocketed. It has been long recognised that the potential of new educational technologies is enormous and as well yet to fully manifest. New technologies allow for a new type of teaching and learning environments, freeing professors, and students from the chains of the classroom (factory). Digital natives who learn in new virtual settings expect fluidity, adaptability and teaching that is student-centred. Students will demand these new learning approaches and through websites such as ratemyteacher.com, will expect them. Indeed, due to the pandemic virtual education has gone from a question that needed to be eventually addressed to an urgent and immediate concern.

But the shift is not only about educational technology. It is also about a new model of pedagogy which is likely to morph into a facilitative model of teaching and learning that is far more student-centred and flexible. In this emergent model, the teacher uses new technologies for lectures – the flipped classroom – and classroom time for discussions. He or she then does not need to know all the answers; rather, he or she facilitates the discussion. This is done by encouraging students to focus on problems that are compelling and urgent to them. They engage in inquiry. The teacher/professor still provides the content architecture but does not require students to memorize or engage in rote learning. They solve problems. The professor then moves to the role of knowledge navigator, helping students find their content pathways. The student is first. The factory transforms into the playground where learning becomes fun. If education is to be improved, the role of teacher will need to shift as well. This is because teacher enthusiasm has most strongly (and positively) been associated with students' performance (OECD, 2019).

Deepening the Analysis

Using the Causal layered analysis approach to unpacking reality and offering alternatives, education in the future could move from one size fits all to a tailored approach. Numerous schools hope to create this reality within a decade.

CLA ON EDUCATION FUTURES	TODAY	PREFERRED FUTURE
Litany description	Mandatory schooling. Standardized, outdated, restricted.	Flexible, unrestricted, global. Everyone has access. Relevant and adaptable.
The system	Segregated by status and gender. Restricted. Does not support individuality.	Students control learning. Increasing drive to learn. Increasing access to education.
The worldview	Recall and striving for results rather than knowledge.	Knowledge is useful and adaptive.
The myth-metaphor	Generic suit	Tailor-made suit

Another key factor is the shift from competition to cooperation. Here as well, students scored higher when they also reported greater co-operation amongst their peers (OECD, 2019). Finally, developing a "growth mindset" has also been "positively associated with students' motivation to master tasks, general self-efficacy, setting learning goals and perceiving the value of school; it was negatively associated with their fear of failure" (OECD, 2019: 16).

To do this well, the emotional intelligence of the professor is critical. Helping students engage in cooperative learning – working together – is central. And metrics need to be designed to reward such behaviour instead of rewarding "the individual hero" – from what is in it for me to we are in this together. Indeed, it will no longer be sufficient to simply "ace" key aspects of the curriculum. For example, "15-year-old students in four provinces/municipalities of China – Beijing, Shanghai, Jiangsu and Zhejiang – outperformed their peers in all of the other 78 participating education systems – in mathematics and science by a wide margin, and in reading, only Singapore came close" (Schleicher, 2018: 5). At the same time, "they have a long way to go when it comes to improving the social and emotional outcomes, and other aspects of students' well-being … areas where other countries excel (ibid).

More balanced approaches to education are going to be increasingly needed in the future. Indeed, participants at a month-long futures course/workshop in Shanghai suggested a new narrative was needed from the current education in China metaphorically described "as a zoo". They wished to see learning and teaching transform to "an organic orchid" or even to "a Disneyland playground". The first is more nature based with learning while the second is more concerned about virtual play – fun!

CLA ON EDUCATION FUTURES - CHINA	TODAY	2040
Litany description	Institutional school education	Multiple approaches: formal, informal and peer to peer
The system	Compulsory education with passive students	Flexible and diversified pathways
The worldview	Good education leads to a good job which leads a successful life	Learning about the self, the world, and the future
The myth-metaphor	The dragon bounded by the great all	The dragon pulling China to a globalized education

In futures work with senior educational leaders in China, they too saw the fundamental need to become far more flexible. For them, seeing this from the view of the national development, they suggested the country needed to leave the boundaries of the great wall and become far more global.

In Norway, they discussed moving from the education as a "factory/castle" to a "jazz orchestra", where there is individual excellence, but cooperation is the key. The role of the educational system is to ensure inner and outer harmony (Inayatullah, 2020a). Other Ministries of Education have responded with narrative such as the "wrecking ball" (Inayatullah, 2020a) – that is the system cannot be transformed and must be destroyed.

Many organisations and individuals have long recognised that foundational change is needed. UNESCO (2021), for example, has been progressively releasing reports to "address the challenges the future holds and to inspire change and issue policy recommendations for education". Starting in 1971-1972, the first of these reports was entitled *Learning to Be: The World of Education Today and Tomorrow*. This was followed by *Learning: The Treasure Within* in 1996. The latter report emphasized "the four pillars" of education: learning to be, learning to know, learning to do, and learning to live together. In 2021, UNESCO released a report based on the fifth pillar of learning to become. The report is based on a broader set of initiatives aimed at rethinking education and shaping the future. Together with efforts in futures literacy (Miller, 2018), the global initiative is to catalyse the debate on how "knowledge, education and learning need to be reimagined in a world of increasing complexity, uncertainty, and precarity" (UNESCO, 2021).

Businesses and emerging industries are further leading in this area, and they may pressure universities to adopt pedagogies that are more relevant, that lead to the skills and competencies they require. Some of those competencies include critical, innovative, and adaptive thinking, emotional and social intelligence, new media literacy, networking, transdisciplinary skills, and virtual collaboration skills. It is a facilitative model of learning, rather than the traditional hierarchical one, that can best assist students develop such needed skills and personal attributes for a changing future. This may help reverse the situation in which, currently, two thirds of the university students are "chasing careers that won't exist" as early as of 2030 (Brown, 2015). Education may further be disrupted by the major players – Alibaba, Google, and Facebook – offering degree courses not just for their employees but the broader public as well. Of course, national accreditation will work against this trend, however, there may be enhanced pressures for the accreditation barrier to be broken.

The Government of Malaysia recognizing these changes developed four futures of education (Inayatullah, 2020b; Ministry of Education, 2018).

NO CHANGE
TRADITIONAL BRICK & MORTAR UNIVERSITY

Universities choose to engage in "business as usual" mode in delivery of education and dependency on the government for financial assistance. The traditional brick and mortar university may have the tendency of not responding to the demands of 4IR. However, it will undergo minimal changes in order to remain relevant and sustainable. Innovative approaches to partnership and collaboration between universities and industries will materialise but will less likely be sustainable in the long run.

MARGINAL CHANGE
JUKEBOX UNIVERSITY

The model allows students to select courses and educational programmes from various institutions using a concept similar to a musical 'jukebox'. The certification is awarded by the universities that have mutual recognitions on the programmes offered.

FUTURE UNIVERSITY MODEL

ADAPTIVE CHANGE
UBERISED UNIVERSITY

This type of university model provides cost-effective education through learning platforms. This model mimics the Uber urban transportation service concept whereby education is demand-driven, self-tailored, hassle free, highly accessible and convenient. The focus of this model is flexible education which promotes access to lifelong learning.

RADICAL CHANGE
NANO/MICRO CERTIFICATION

Nano/Micro certification model is a non-traditional certification programme offered by organisations/individuals that is recognised by the industry. It uses modular concept where certifications and credentials are stackable. These industry-driven certifications are capturing the interest of the digital natives.

The first was the conventional "Bricks and Mortar," with few choices for students. The second was the "Jukebox University," with students having far greater choices in courses. The third, the adaptive scenario, was called the "Uberification of Education," with students able to call education to them, anytime, from anywhere. The final, the radical scenario, was "Nano-education and certification," with continuous micro-accreditation being an integral aspect of lifelong learning.

While most focus on the first two scenarios the last two suggest dramatic changes ahead. In the uberification scenario, students can learn anytime, from anywhere, and most significantly from anyone. These portents the potential death of the university. The imagination of H. G. Wells (1938) and the global brain, all having possible equal access suddenly seams realizable.

The final scenario of nano-education takes the debate further, challenging the formal nation-state based accreditation system. Nations and regions could still accredit but the process would be skill by skill, course by course. Students would design their life educational futures. Accreditation would also not just be national but as with Trip Advisor and Airbnb, there would be far more ptp involvement. The university would be one of many providers.

The future also moves away from the physical and toward the metaverse with professors becoming holograms. Immersive technologies would sit aside green technologies. Thus, there would be not just flexibility of courses but as well the medium in which one learns and whom one learns with.

This means a world where learning is where you want it, when you want it, how you want it, at a cheaper cost, with novel forms of certification. Already, we are seeing the advent of predictive avatars and coaches in the Healthcare industry via innovation, e.g., as in Nfinity Avatars platform which aims to "bring online service and education fully into the 21st century" (N-Avatars.com, 2021).

Certainly, the costs and benefits will be felt differently across various regions. While some societies will continue to benefit from the "demographic dividend", others may experience enhanced social conflict due to the "youth bulge" if it is coupled with inequity, unemployment, and disempowerment of the younger generations (Inayatullah, 2016). Equity and spending on education have also long been recognised as an issue impacting education. Gaps have consistently been observed between socio-economically advantaged and disadvantaged students. For example, on average, socio economically advantaged students outperformed their disadvantaged peers by 75 points in reading, equivalent to 2-2.5 years of schooling (World Bank, 2018). Inequity has risen because of the COVID-19 pandemic, and we can anticipate that it will continue to negatively impact education in the future.

A positive relationship between performance and per student spending is currently jeopardised due to the economic fallout from the pandemic. However, this driver will likely push education to find ways to further enhance effectiveness and design alternative approaches to teaching and learning. Such new models which would offer a considerable cost savings and enhance mobility have already been in development (Inayatullah & Milojević, 2016; Milojević & Inayatullah, 2018).

Still, for the new model to succeed issues of social justice will need to be addressed (Inayatullah and Milojević, 2016). Of particular concern is the number of girls abandoning formal education, leading to decades long gains being reversed. It is estimated that twenty percent of girls in East Asia and the Pacific, or close to 40 million of them in total, have not been able to access distance learning during COVID-19, whilst nearly 69 percent reported studying and learning less than usual (The Diplomat, 2020). In South and West Asia, "2.8 million women and girls may not be able to return to education, from pre-primary to tertiary levels" (The Diplomat, 2020). Like virtual education, equity issues would thus also move from being a question that needed to be eventually addressed to an urgent and immediate concern.

References and Further Reading

Babb, J. & Buchanan, N. (2020). *COVID-19 Leaves Millions of Girls at Risk of School Dropout in Asia-Pacific*. The Diplomat. https://thediplomat.com/2020/11/covid-19-leaves-millions-of-girls-at-risk-of-school-dropout-in-asia-pacific/

Bhattacharjee, R. & Siyahirah, J. S. (2018). Missing Skills: Is Higher Education on the Mark. *The Edge Malaysia*, Issue 19 - 25 February 2018.

Brown, R. (2015, August 24). *'More than half' of students chasing dying careers*. ABC News. http://www.abc.net.au/ news/2015-08-24/next-generation-chasing-dying-careers/6720528

The Economist (2017, July 22). *Special Issue on the Future of Learning: How Technology is Transforming education*. The Economist.

Inayatullah, S. (2016). The Youth Bulge. *Journal of Futures Studies*, 21(2): 21-24.

Inayatullah, S. (2020a). *Co-Creating Educational Futures: Contradictions Between the Emerging Future and the Walled Past. Education Research and Foresight*. Working Paper 27. Paris: UNESCO.

Inayatullah, S. (2020b). Scenarios for Teaching and Training. *CSPS Strategy and Policy Journal,* (8): 31-48.

Inayatullah, S. & Milojević, I. (2016). Leadership and Governance in Higher Education: Can Malaysian Universities Meet the Challenge. *Foresight,* 18: 434-440.

Inayatullah, S. & Na, L. (2018). *Asia 2038: Ten Disruptions That Change Everything*. Taipei: Tamkang University Press.

Inayatullah, S & Ithnin, F. (2018). *Transformation 2050: The Alternative Futures of Malaysian Universities*. Bandar Baru Nila: Universiti Sains Islam Malaysia.

Marshman, I. & Larkins, F. (2021). *COVID-19: What Australian Universities Can Do to Recover from the Loss of International Student Fees*. The Conversation. https://theconversation.com/covid-19-what-australian-universities-can-do-to-recover-from-the-loss-of-international-student-fees-139759

Milojević, I. (2003). Will We Ever Learn: What Sort of Education Do We Need for the Future? *Social Alternatives*, 22(4): 17–21.

Milojević, I. (2011). *Educational Futures: Dominant and Contesting Visions*. 2nd edition (paperback). London: Routledge.

Milojević, I. & Inayatullah, S. (2018). From Skiling for New Futures to Empowering Individuals and Communities. *Journal of Futures Studies*, 22 (4): 1–14.

Ministry of Education (2018). *Framing Malaysian Higher Education 4.0*. Putrajaya: Government of Malaysia.

N-Avatars.Com (2021). https://n-avatars.com/the-avatar-advantage/

OECD (2019). *PISA 2018 Results: Combined Executive Summaries*. OECD. http://www.oecd.org/pisa/Combined_Executive_Summaries_PISA_2018.pdf

Schleicher, A. (2018). *PISA 2018: Insights and Interpretations*. OECD. http://www.oecd.org/pisa/PISA%202018%20Insights%20and%20Interpretations%20FINAL%20PDF.pdf

UNESCO (2021). *UNESCO Global Reports on Education*. Paris: UNESCO. https://en.unesco.org/futuresofeducation/initiative.

Well, H. (1938). *World Brain* (1st ed.). Garden City, N.Y.: Doubleday, Doran & Co.

World Bank Group (2018). *PISA 2018: East Asia and Pacific Region*. http://documents1.worldbank.org/curated/en/876861593415668827/pdf/East-Asia-and-Pacific-Regional-Brief-Programme-for-International-Student-Assessment-PISA-2018.pdf

Zhou. N. (2021). *More than 17,000 Jobs Lost at Australian Universities During COVID Pandemic*. The Guardian. https://www.theguardian.com/australia-news/2021/feb/03/more-than-17000-jobs-lost-at-australian-universities-during-covid-pandemic

99

Authors

Sohail Inayatullah

Sohail Inayatullah, a political scientist and futurist, is the UNESCO Chair in Futures Studies at the Sejahtera Centre for Sustainability and Humanity, Malaysia. He is also Professor at Tamkang University, Taiwan and Associate, Melbourne Business School, the University of Melbourne. He teaches from www.metafutureschool.org. For 2021, he was virtual futurist-in-residence with the government of Abu Dhabi, Culture and Tourism.

His most recent book is *Asia 2038* (in English, Mandarin, and Korean) and with the Asian Development Bank, *Futures Thinking in Asia and the Pacific: Why foresight matters for policymaker*s (2020).

In the last year and a half, he has worked with the Government of New Zealand; WHO; the Government of Egypt; The Asian Development Bank; Globe Telecom; ISESCO in Tunisia; Queensland Police; EDOTCO, Malaysia; the Office of the President, the Government of Argentina; Impact Investment, Brazil; the Korean Development Institute; the United Nations Economic and Social Commission of Asia and the Pacific; INTERPOL; the Philippines Senate; the National Disabilities Services; Edmund Rice Education Australia; Powerlink, Queensland; Brisbane Grammar School, Queensland; Walter and Eliza Hall Institute for Medical Research, Australia; the Australia Tax Organization; Groupo Zap, Brazil; the Korean Global Forum for Peace, and, Gurukul International.

Ivana Milojević

Ivana Milojević is a researcher, writer and educator with a trans-disciplinary professional background in sociology, education, gender, peace and futures studies. She obtained her BA degree in sociology at the University of Belgrade in 1992 and a PhD in education at the University of Queensland in 2003.

Since the mid-1990s, she has delivered speeches and facilitated workshops for governmental institutions, international associations, and non-governmental organizations in Australia, Asia-Pacific (Brunei Darussalam, Iran, Malaysia, Pakistan, South Korea, Taiwan, UAE, and US-Hawaii), South Africa, and Europe (Croatia, Belgium, Denmark, Finland, France, Hungary, Italy, Serbia, Sweden, Switzerland, and Turkey). She was previously a professor at several universities (The University of the Sunshine Coast, Australia (Adjunct Professor, 2009-2015), University of Novi Sad, Serbia (Visiting Professor, 2008-ongoing) and Tamkang University, Taiwan (2015)). In 2016-2017 she led the foresight unit at the Centre for Strategic and Policy Studies, Brunei Darussalam. She is currently the Director of Metafuture, a global think-tank and the Metafuture School, an online platform for futures courses. In addition to policy reports, academic books and journal articles she also writes fiction - her most recent books include *The Future Maker* and *The Gold Maker*, available at www.tales.metafuture.org

Contact

Metafuture
https://www.metafuture.org/
info@metafuture.org

Metafuture School
https://www.metafutureschool.org/
adam@metafutureschool.org

Sohail Inayatullah
sinayatullah@gmail.com

Ivana Milojević
ivana@metafuture.org

Published 2022 by Metafuture.org

The End of the Cow and Other Emerging Issues

ISBN 978-0-6453461-5-2